You're On Your Way!

CLARA O'NEAL

WestBow Press books may be ordered through booksellers or by contacting:

WestBow Press
A Division of Thomas Nelson & Zondervan
1663 Liberty Drive
Bloomington, IN 47403
www.westbowpress.com
844.714.3454

Because of the dynamic nature of the Internet, any web addresses or links contained in this book may have changed since publication and may no longer be valid. The views expressed in this work are solely those of the author and do not necessarily reflect the views of the publisher, and the publisher hereby disclaims any responsibility for them.

Any people depicted in stock imagery provided by Getty Images are models, and such images are being used for illustrative purposes only.
Certain stock imagery © Getty Images.

Interior Image Credit: Madison Pha Snook

ISBN: 978-1-6642-0411-9 (sc)
ISBN: 978-1-6642-0413-3 (hc)
ISBN: 978-1-6642-0412-6 (e)

Library of Congress Control Number: 2020916581

Print information available on the last page.

WestBow Press rev. date: 05/22/2021

You're On Your Way!

You're on your way...

Today is your day.

It's time to celebrate YOU!

You've done great work.

You've made it through,

·REPORT CARD·

Math A+

English A+

Science A+

History A+

and here's the golden question...

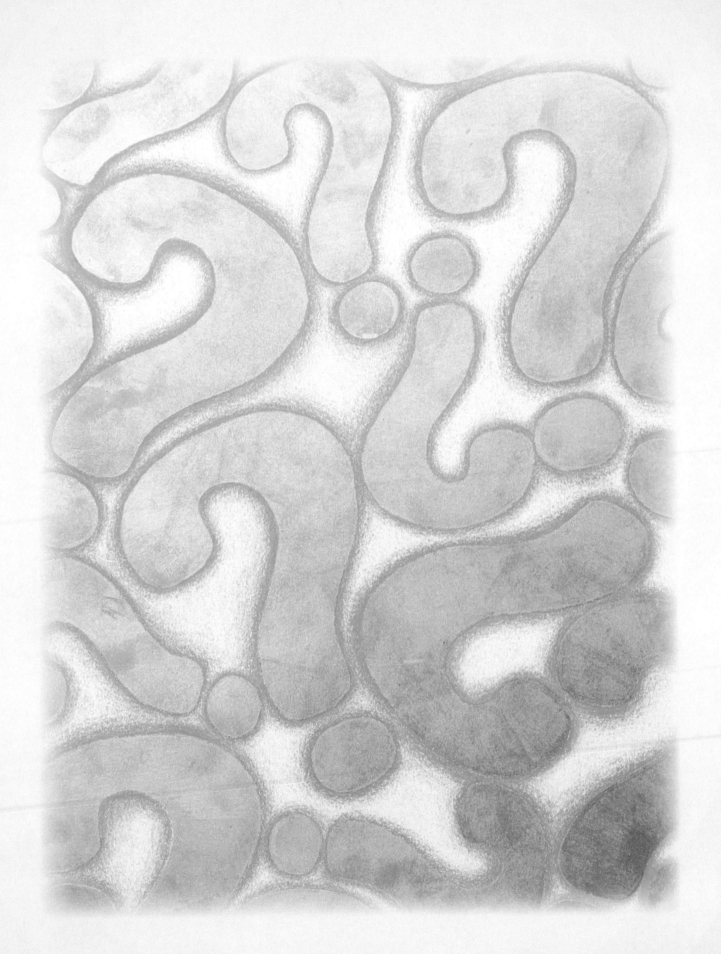

Now what will you do?

You're special, you're talented,

and creative; it's true.

But this next chapter in life...

is driven by YOU!

Be honest, be kind, be gracious too.

Never think there is anything
you can't put your heart to.

Some doors will be opened.

Other doors will close.

Putting others first is how
the story should go.

Know that you are loved
and cared for a lot.

Face the world each day,
and give it all you've got.

Challenges will be endless, and they will always be there.

So remain strong in your faith, knowing God is ALWAYS near.

Printed in the United States
by Baker & Taylor Publisher Services